Home of the Brave
OR HOW TO OVERTHROW
THE TYRANNY OF STUFF

A Life Guide

Libby Wood

This book is dedicated to my wonderful clients, some of whom the reader will meet in these pages. Thank you for letting me be a part of your life.

CONTENTS

❧ The Problem ❧

We are drowning in our own stuff. We have so many posses-
sions that they bog us down. They get in our way, they distract us,
and they create stress in our lives.

This problem affects not just Americans; it's a worldwide issue. A
2014 book, *The Life-Changing Magic of Tidying Up: The Japanese Art
of Decluttering and Organizing* by Marie Kondo, became a #1 best-
seller. She even had a television program. Margareta Magnussen made
a big splash with *The Gentle Art of Swedish Death Cleaning* at the end
of 2017. If you haven't read those books or seen the TV show, I recommend them.

My company is called "Get Libby Now!" and I've been working
on the front lines of this issue for several years. I've worked with
hoarders and I've worked with people who just needed someone to
help sort it all out. Most of them agree that the stuff is a problem,
but they can't deal with it alone. Along the way I've gained a few
insights into the sources of the problem, and I have some suggestions
about ways to get the upper hand on all that stuff.

Both Marie and Margareta have valuable perspectives, but my
own perspective is American. I believe that as Americans, we share
a common outlook that is important to consider. By and large, we
value self-sufficiency, individualism, and independence. We want to
"paddle our own canoes" to the very end of our lives, and we don't
want to be dependent upon anyone else. That matters.

Marie's book promotes an almost mystical relationship between a person and his or her stuff. She starts each job by talking to the house. Every day she thanks her own belongings for giving her joy. Americans might appreciate this perspective and find it interesting, but I have trouble imagining that very many of us have taken her advice that far. She does have practical suggestions, however, such as the way she folds and stores clothes in drawers, that are useful and easy to implement.

Margareta's approach is more about leaving your family a beautiful bequest by preparing for death in a thoughtful way. When I was younger, I held on to many, many things with the thought that my heirs would one day find them wonderful. Now, after having witnessed one inheritance after another in which the heirs have had to resort to hiring junk haulers, my own perspective is more in line with Margareta's. Those heirs almost universally want far less than they actually inherit.

But, while death cleaning might motivate Swedes, Americans might prefer to focus on the present. I don't see us spending a lot of time worrying about whether our grown children will really want that seven-foot-tall statue of Neptune. (My sister really did inherit such a thing from our mother's cousin. Fortunately, that cousin had a neighbor who had always admired that statue. It was a classic win-win solution. I prefer not to think about the neighbor's heirs.)

For several years I had a window office in a high-rise on Market Street in the Financial District of San Francisco. Many of my coworkers were Chinese Americans, so the Facilities Department had a staff member trained in Feng Shui (pronounced "fung shwee"), a way of harmonizing individuals with their environments, a practice that is more than six thousand years old. The structural pole in the middle of that office was a challenge, but she did the best she could. My favorite of her recommendations was that I should always keep pink flowers on my desk.

Even if one doesn't subscribe to the metaphysical aspects of

Feng Shui, the quest for balance and harmony in one's environment is universal. Keeping that environment free of unnecessary items is a common thread.

Just about every culture has dealt with this issue, both now and in the past. For Americans, freedom and independence resonate, and we achieve both as we lighten our loads and eliminate items that weigh us down in our homes and in our lives. This book is an exploration of ways to go about that: by an American, for Americans.

❧ Our Fears ❧

Let's start by identifying potential sources of the problem. Why is acquiring things so much easier than releasing them? Acquiring them is expensive and releasing them is relatively cheap. What drives us to surround ourselves with an uncomfortable and even unhealthy amount of stuff?

My contention is that the underlying source of this tendency is often fear. But before we break down some of the different types of fears that can feed into the "stuff" problem, let's be clear. Fear is not a character flaw. It's not a sin. It's not even politically incorrect. It just happens. Being brave does not mean the absence of fear. It just means that we face those fears and deal with them.

Now let's wade in there and tear apart a few of the most common fears.

❧ Thrift ❧

"A penny saved is a penny earned" – *Benjamin Franklin* *

Not only do we want to hang on to our pennies, we think that we need to hang on to our things to avoid having to buy those same things again at some later date.

Of course, thrift itself is a great thing. However, old Ben didn't suggest that last week's Sunday newspaper saved is a penny earned. He was talking about money. He was saying that we should evaluate whether or not we really use and value that newspaper and that if we don't, then we should eliminate the subscription.

We need to be realistic about what stuff is worth saving. Will we really fix that old appliance, put it up for sale, take phone calls from potential buyers, then wait at home for them to come and evaluate the item's condition? Or should we let the recycling center deal with it?

I once ran across a case of inexpensive bourbon in the basement of a client's house. I'll call her Heloise. (I've changed the names of all of my clients in this book to protect their privacy.) I asked her why it was there, since I knew she didn't particularly like any kind of whiskey. She told me that she and her husband had bought it years ago because a regular guest in their house had liked that brand. It was still there because that friend had died 20 years earlier, before he had a chance to drink any of it. Rather

---

* *He actually wrote, "A penny saved is two pence clear" and not "A penny saved is a penny earned" but let's not quibble.*

than toss it or give it away, Heloise had stashed it there in case some other guest sometime wanted some of that bourbon.

The irony here is that not only was Heloise quite wealthy, she was also very generous. She would not have hesitated to buy a case of better bourbon for any guest. She had probably done that in the intervening years. But she kept that particular case of bourbon all those years, on the off chance that someone else might prefer that brand.

This illustrates the fear that we might be giving up something that will turn out to be useful someday. The truth is that this fear is valid; the possibility exists. But what are the actual chances of our needing that thing? What would be the cost of replacing it? Also, is it perishable? Is it subject to the whims of fashion? Heloise recognized the low probability of that case of liquor being useful and knew she needed to downsize, so she had no problem letting it go when I prompted her.

Steve saved golf balls. In his retirement years he worked part time at a golf course. Each night, before going home, he would stuff golf balls into his pockets. When his widow hired me to help her deal with his stuff, we found an entire closet of shoe boxes filled with used golf balls. These folks easily had the means to buy as many golf balls as he needed, naturally.

My favorite example of false economy comes not from my current business but from when I was managing people in San Francisco. I had an employee call in sick one day. He told me that he really wasn't sick, so I asked him for the story. He reluctantly told me that the previous day he had gone to a warehouse store and bought several economy-size bottles of maple syrup, which he put in the pantry off of his dining room. Overnight, the shelf in the pantry broke, the bottles shattered, and the maple syrup soaked the carpet in the dining room and on down through to the subfloor. Those were some very expensive bottles of maple syrup.

❧ Sense of Identity ❧

"You can take away everything a man has
as long as you leave him his dignity" – John Wayne

How does this relate to our stuff? Sometimes our stuff helps define us.

Walter's house had beautiful tile and woodwork that he had installed himself. While his house was quite comfortable, the basement was out of control. It was jam-packed. The rat droppings were ankle-deep, and as he and I worked through the stuff, we uncovered dead rats.

Walter was dealing with some serious health issues that had their origins when he was a soldier in Viet Nam. But his life had been characterized by a series of adventures. His "stuff" included camping, fishing, and hunting equipment, horse paraphernalia, mechanics' tools, sound and photography equipment, and so on. He had been competent in a wide range of activities, most of which were closed to him when I met him due to his health.

For Walter, letting go of that stuff meant acknowledging that he would never again repair a tractor or hunt a bear. It meant letting go of part of himself. In the end, he retained quite a bit of stuff that he honestly expects he won't use again. But we did eliminate several truckloads of stuff, and what remains is clean and organized. The rats and their droppings are gone, as are the items that attracted them in the first place. When Walter decides to go further, the job will be much easier.

Renee's case was similar. She and her husband had once owned a large home with lots of beautiful furniture. But his business failed and shortly thereafter he died, so she moved to a much smaller apartment and put most of that furniture in storage. After 15 years of paying for storage, she finally came to terms with the idea that her old life was in the past and her new life in a smaller place characterizes who she is now.

A variation on this theme is illustrated by Brenda. Her husband had been a local celebrity when he passed away, so eliminating his stuff felt to her like erasing him from the history books. Fortunately, in her case, a local museum was able to accept several boxes of memorabilia, some of which is now on display. Sometimes, the sense of identity is about a spouse or a parent.

❧ Sentimentality ☙

"Sentimentality is the emotional promiscuity of those who have no sentiment" – *Norman Mailer*

When everything is sentimental, nothing is.

I was contacted by Edgar, who was interested in my services. I met with Edgar and his wife, Janelle. He was enthusiastic about engaging my services. She was not.

Edgar and Janelle had a very large house, but it was jammed full of stuff. One of the big issues was the dining room, which was filled, floor to ceiling, with stacks of Janelle's deceased mother's furniture. No one could enter that room. Edgar wanted his dining room back.

Janelle felt that getting rid of her mother's furniture was disrespectful. She didn't want to use her mom's furniture because she already had her own, which she preferred, but she wanted to just keep all of mom's stuff. As far as I know, that furniture is still there, because Edgar and Janelle couldn't agree on what to do about it. (So much for my career in marriage counselling.)

The first problem with Janelle's thinking is that her mother would not have wanted her furniture to end up in an unused stack. Secondly, having so many mementos dilutes the impact of each item. If Janelle could have selected one or two cherished items and showcased them in her home, she and Edgar would have appreciated them and remembered her mom in a positive

9

way. Instead, Janelle's relationship with Edgar suffers because of her mom's stuff.

Janelle was afraid that getting rid of that furniture would mean that she was getting rid of her memories of her mom.

Several of my clients have called me shortly after a death in the family, usually a parent or a spouse. Often, their emotions are an impediment to action, but they feel the need to deal with the stuff for either financial or emotional reasons.

Folk wisdom says that a widow or widower shouldn't make any big decisions until a year after the spouse's death, which is a valid guideline to consider. But Heloise made the decision to move just a few months after her husband's death, and she never regretted it.

Heloise had had a solid marriage that had lasted for a very long time and resulted in four wonderful children. But moving gave her the space to define herself as an individual, rather than half of a couple. Every marriage involves compromises, and one of the compromises that Heloise made had to do with a couple of blue sofas in her living room that she had always hated, but that her husband had loved. Those sofas, along with a several truck-loads of other items, were not included in the interior design for the new house. That new house is decorated utterly in Heloise's style, which is very distinctive and very artistic, but definitely not the same as her husband's style.

Brenda had a similar experience. Because her husband had a big personality, his belongings dominated the house while he was alive, and she had suppressed her some of her artistic instincts. When he passed away, she went a little bit wild and filled every inch of available space with art objects and artificial plants. I was brought in by her realtor to help clear some space so that potential buyers could imagine themselves living in the home.

The items that Brenda used to decorate her home were lovely, so using them to stage the home was easy. The problem was that she had more than twice as many items as the house could comfortably hold. She had a large basement, but it was already filled with items that she had tried and rejected. So, our first step was to clear the basement so that the extraneous items from upstairs could be put there.

Initially, the process was difficult. Brenda wanted every item exactly where she had placed it. A few times we would agree that an item could go to the basement, so down it went. Then the next day I would find it upstairs again. But as time went on, Brenda began to see beauty in having space between the items. After a few days, she told me, "I'm starting to understand what you're getting at. I see it now, and I want you to come to my new house and help me put it together this same way."

The good news is that Brenda still calls me periodically and I help her clear out a couple of items that have become clutter. Then we go and have a nice lunch together.

❧ Guilt ❦

"Guilt – the gift that keeps on giving" – Erma Bombeck

Fear of guilt has kept some of the worst junk in my clients' homes.

Well-meaning children and grandchildren had given my client Marcella so much stuff that every surface was completely covered. The sofa and chairs in her living room were covered with so many pillows that she had no place to sit. She had so many storage containers that she had blocked the door to the master bedroom and had to go in and out through the bathroom. But she was worried about getting rid of things that her children or grandchildren had given her. She was afraid she'd feel...guilty.

Holding on to those gifts may seem like the way to express appreciation for them, but it really isn't. Marcella's children were frustrated with the state of her home. They wanted her to be more comfortable and less stressed. They probably couldn't have picked out their individual gifts among all that clutter and weren't really interested in checking up on their gifts, anyway.

I've had this same conversation with my own mother. She had a little musical teapot that her mother-in-law, my grandmother, had given her many, many years ago. Mom had never liked the style of that teapot and the tune was downright annoying to her, but she kept it because she didn't want to feel guilty about giving it away. She never used it and kept it in the back of an inaccessible cupboard. Even after Grandma passed away, Mom kept the teapot. She held on to it for several more decades, until I helped her move into a senior community at age 90. Even then, giving that thing up was a struggle for her.

Choosing a gift is difficult, and sometimes the only present that comes to mind is similar to something that the recipient already has: Surely Mom would like another teapot, she was so devoted tom the one Grandma gave her! Honestly, though, if Mom releases that teapot to someone else who might love it, that doesn't mean that the thought wasn't appreciated.

❧ Insecurity ☙

The good news about a collection is that the family can almost always find a gift for a collector. The bad news is that usually no one else wants that collection.

How is a collection driven by fear? Collecting doesn't stem from being afraid, exactly, but from an underlying insecurity. In my experience, collectors are often filling some kind of void. They have a need to feel that sense of satisfaction that comes with each addition to the collection. They want that feeling of accomplishment that they don't get in other ways. So they focus their energy on collecting, which gives them that sure-fire hit of gratification every time they find a new piece.

For me, the most troublesome type of collecting is what I think of as icon-based. As long as the item has a duck on it, for example, it belongs in the collection, regardless of the quality, attractiveness, or utility of the item. In some way this type of collecting is done to define the collector's personality, to identify the person with the image of the duck, or whatever. So the idea of releasing that collection triggers the fear of losing one's identity.

Another type of collecting, which is marginally more sensible, is collecting with the expectation that the price of the items will rise extravagantly over time. Although some collectors do make money, in order to do so the collector has to be very good at anticipating trends. This is like trying to time the stock market. What's popular today may or may not be popular tomorrow, and the trick is to predict those market changes accurately.

My mother's mother was born in 1904, and the only thing she inherited from her mother was a small bowl of carnival glass. That bowl was the start of Grandma's carnival-glass-collecting mania. She bought pieces. We gave her pieces. Other people of her generation also collected carnival glass, which drove the price up outrageously. Then, that generation began to pass away. The price of carnival glass fell through the floor. Younger generations consider the stuff unattractive. Today, it sits on shelves at Goodwill and Salvation Army stores. My sister has that one small piece that belonged to our great-grandmother, and I can't say that I am jealous.

My client Martha collected Barbie dolls. Unopened boxes of them were in the dining room and living room and in huge stacks in the garage. She had hundreds of them. Unfortunately, Martha was disabled and couldn't walk without help, but she was convinced that someday she would be more able-bodied and that she would sell the dolls for huge amounts of money. However, as things stood when I encountered them, the dolls were an enormous hinderance and of limited monetary value. Today, Martha's sister is valiantly trying to sell them online.

Although my clients often think that collections will become valuable, they almost never do. Stamps, coins, comic books, baseball cards, rocks, cookie jars, teapots, nativity scenes, Barbie dolls, and so on gave those collectors some level of pleasure during the accumulation process. Occasionally they do escalate for a time: Beanie Babies, Dutch tulip bulbs, postage stamps, and baseball cards have had their day. But my clients have rarely seen their collections appreciate over the years, and their heirs are almost never fighting to inherit those collections.

15

❧ Solutions ❧

So, if Americans are so independent and self-sufficient, why do we let our fears drive us to the point of drowning in our own stuff? Better yet, how can we gather our courage and deal with it?

My mom is an extraordinary person. She graduated from high school at age 14 and was the first person in her family to go to college, even though her parents didn't see why she should bother. When she got there, she applied to the math department to major in math. The department chair told her that girls weren't allowed in the department. She persisted and finally got him to agree that if she took physics and chemistry first, and did well, then he'd consider allowing her to study math. She did that, and in time he became her mentor and friend.

Today, such a situation is almost unthinkable. We encourage girls to study math and science. We go out of our way to give them every advantage. Yet, girls are still underrepresented in those fields. This is incomprehensible to Mom. Once, she was interviewed by my friend who was writing a book on inspiring women. My friend asked Mom, "What advice would you give girls today?" The question threw Mom for a loop. The obstacles she had to overcome are gone and so now she can't understand why more girls don't want to study math. "Just do it," she told the author.

My own approach to the problem of stuff reflects a lot of Mom's attitude. We can think about it. We can talk about it. We can tiptoe around it. But, if we really want it done, we've just got to do it.

Hollywood gives us plenty of examples of characters who get things done that way. We have action heroes and superheroes. We have westerns, with the guy in the white hat saving the day all by himself. We have Dirty Harry. We have Captain America. We have hundreds of potential role models.

*"Sometimes if you want to see a change for the better,
you have to take things into your own hands" – Clint Eastwood*

That's my message. Take the bull by the horns. Jump in with both feet. Bite the bullet. Just do it.

Back to the math topic. My degree is also in math, and I sometimes take on private math students. I find that the best predictor of who will do well in math isn't native intelligence or some inherited "math gene." It is simply a modicum of intelligence, lots of diligence, a bit of self-discipline, and some basic organizational skills. The same is true when it comes to dealing with our stuff.

We live in an age of outsourcing. We eat packaged, prepared food. We watch professionals play games for us. We get our teeth cleaned and our nails polished. These are all wonderful things. But dealing with the stuff is something each of us has to tackle personally. We can get help, but it's our stuff.

Occasionally, a client will come to me with the idea that I can clear out the stuff on my own, without his or her input. The truth is that all I can do is point out problems, make suggestions, and carry out the client's decisions. The client has to do that hard work of MAKING those decisions.

Self-reliance is a bedrock American characteristic. I grew up in Bakersfield, California among the displaced Dust Bowl Okies who populated that town at that time. My own parents and grandparents were part of that group of people. Yet *The Grapes of Wrath*, the classic book by John Steinbeck, which documented that time and place, was a very unpopular book there

One problem they had with *The Grapes of Wrath* was the way it characterizes the migrants as ignorant, slow-witted victims, which they found insulting. In my own experience this is about as far from the truth as possible. I knew them to be clever, hard-working, and very self-reliant. It is a well-written book, certainly, but it missed the mark there.

The book also promotes the idea that the only way out of bad situations is to share what little is available, which is completely contrary to that group's attitude. The philosophy I learned from them was that I should work as hard as I can at whatever is in front of me, and if that doesn't work, to try something else and work as hard as I can at that.

Which is not to say that sharing wasn't important. Those folks were some of the most generous, welcoming people in the world. But they were NOT victims and would never accept charity themselves. To me, that's the essence of being American.

These were also people comfortable with picking up stakes and moving down the road. A few years after the 2008 economic crisis, I heard a panel of economists talking about the recovery, which by that time was well underway. While one of the economists agreed that the recovery was solid overall, she was concerned that it was still holding on in certain geographical pockets.

In other recoveries, most people had chosen to move to wherever the jobs were, which can be healthy for the national economy overall. But in this case, quite a few people in depressed areas were choosing to stay where they were and make use of various government entitlement programs. Sometimes moving to a new home is not just good for the individual, but good for the society as a whole. Plus, moving forces us to look at our stuff and decide what to take with us.

Anyway, that's my message. We may be drowning in stuff, but it's our stuff. It's our responsibility. No one made us collect it. We are Americans. We can fix this.

✒ Identifying Fears ✒

So how do we deal with the fears that got us here? The first step is determining the underlying source of the clutter. Does the accrual of stuff stem from one of the fears related to thrift, sense of identity, sentimentality, guilt, insecurity, or does it come from somewhere else?

One of my most difficult projects was for my client Mabel, who had collapsed in her home and had been removed to another location when I was hired. My job was to deal with her stuff and prepare for her move to a senior community while she recovered.

Mabel's apartment was small, but racks lined every wall, even the bathroom. She had tall bookcases separated by a few feet and spanning the tops of the bookcases were brooms whose handles served as closet poles. The bookcases were totally filled with clothing, art, art supplies, and just plain trash. The walls that were exposed were streaked with feces, maggots lined the shelves in the kitchen, and the carpets were thick with fleas.

One of the most striking things, however, was her collection of sweaters. Mabel had probably 300–400 sweaters, all very similar in style. Many still had their store tags on them. As I got to know her, I learned that as a young nursing student, she had lived through the Blitz in London in 1940–41. Fear can be as obscure as being afraid to be caught outside without a sweater in a cold, rainy city.

Once the fear is identified, it can be harnessed for positive results. My own motivations often come from fear, and my own strategy is to lean into that fear. I try to think through what the worst possible case might be in each eventuality, then see if I can deal with that outcome.

Mabel and I discussed her priorities for what she would need in her new home. She agreed that one sweater of each color would be enough for any possible situation, so that's how I filled the sweater section of her new closet. But before I took the remainder to charity, I checked in with her. She was in tears. She hadn't thought to tell me about the white raincoat that she had just bought. So when I retrieved that for her, she hugged me and cried happy tears. She told me, "You're the only one who understands."

❧ Other Factors ❧

At this point I need to take a step back and point out that fear may not be the only factor involved. Sometimes other issues conspire with our fears to make things that much worse. I'm tempted to call these "fear-adjacent" considerations. Regardless of what they are called, let's dive into those issues for a bit.

Inertia

Dealing with a large amount of stuff is work, it takes time, and it requires a whole lot of energy, both mental and physical. So, for some people, the whole job sinks to the bottom of the priority list: "It's not that bad (yet)."

Inertia can be a result of fear, too. Many clients have said that without me the job would never have been done. Some of them are afraid that they will disrupt the status quo only to find that they hate organizing so much that they will abandon the effort. This can result in a worse mess that the initial one, and that's a genuine danger.

Plenty of books have been written about how to motivate yourself to exercise more, eat healthier foods, and so on. I am not a motivational expert. But whenever I work with clients, they usually start out pretty unmotivated but just desperate enough to hire me. Then, after a session or two, they always admit to enjoying the process, either because my enthusiasm has rubbed off on them, or because of the lift it gives them when they see progress.

So my advice is to start by figuring out some kind of reward system, which I call the "shiny object" approach:

- "After I sort through the stuff on the kitchen counter, then I will relax with a glass of wine."
- "If I donate two boxes of books to the Friends of the Library, then I can come home with one NEW book to read."
- "Once I've eliminated all the clothes in my closet that don't fit, I'll take a long, hot bubble bath."
- "When the garage is clear enough to park a car in it, I'll trade in my old car."

Over time, the process itself becomes more and more fun as the results become evident. When the results become the reward, that shiny object may no longer be necessary.

Another approach is to work with a coach. Until I started doing this professionally, I had trouble understanding why the job even existed. Sorting through stuff and keeping my own house tidy was second nature, a lifelong habit. For me it was easier to do than to NOT do.

But now that I've done this work for a while, I appreciate how hard it is to break lifelong habits. Sometimes a jump-start is really helpful.

Indecision

Another factor to consider is indecisiveness. Quite a few times I've worked with clients who have taken a book off the shelf, looked at it for a while, put it in the "donate" box, taken it out and put it in the "keep" box, taken it out again and put it back up on the shelf.

Megan was a recent widow and her husband had a historically important collection of books and other early American memorabilia. I found a well-known American university interested in obtaining that collection and willing to honor her husband with a plaque or something similar. But she thought she might want to do something else with those items someday, so they are now in a local storage unit, serving no one. Her children or grandchildren will be faced with the same decision.

When this happens, I almost always encourage clients to think a little harder, if possible. What new information will emerge in the future that will make that decision easier? Why not save your future self from having to make what is clearly a difficult decision? What is holding you back from releasing that item to be loved and appreciated by others?

The only time I encourage clients to move items to the "keep" box is when those items have great sentimental value to them. By this, I mean an important scrapbook or an achievement award, for example. I don't mean that rubber duck collection or National Geographic library.

Indecisiveness itself is a type of fear: the fear of making the wrong decision. Will my future self ever regret donating the item? Am I misjudging the value of the item? Could one of my children have an irrational attachment to the item?

The answer to this fear is to recognize that it is just stuff, and stuff is a problem. Yes, we go to a lot of trouble to acquire stuff, but now it's creating stress and it needs to go. The probability of regret is very low, and the satisfaction of less stuff is a sure thing. As long as that thought is in the forefront, progress is possible.

Defeatism

Another requirement for successfully managing mountains of stuff is confidence that the task is achievable. Starting the project with the mindset that doing it is impossible becomes a self-fulfilling prophecy. The belief that the task is beyond reach means that it is. "I just can't do it."

The answer to this type of defeatism is to take a tiny step. If it doesn't go well, rather than taking that as a sign that the whole thing is impossible, a better approach is to view that experience as a valuable lesson learned on the path to getting the whole project done. Then repeat. And repeat. And repeat.

Similarly, if we see ourselves as hoarders or slobs, and firmly believe that these are fixed aspects of our personalities, then we will fail to defeat the tyranny of stuff. Our personalities become fairly well set early in life, and we adopt certain characteristics at that point, investing quite a bit of energy into some of those characteristics. Unless we allow ourselves to redefine those characteristics, we will defeat our own efforts, either consciously or subconsciously.

I have a couple of things to say about this. First, most of my clients have been somewhere on the hoarder spectrum when I met them. But, after working with me for a while, most of them shifted away from where they were. So, clearly, "hoardishness" and "slobocity" are not genetic, like being tall or short. They are patterns we have learned, and we can replace them with new patterns.

Second, sometimes it is easier to redefine what we consider to be an integral part of our personalities when we have role models who have already done just that. The difficult step here is finding the right mentor who can provide advice about exactly how people who consider themselves hoarders or slobs can become organized. The key is to strongly identify with the successful person.

Finally, defeatism can come from working with the wrong motivation. If we are undertaking this project for some reason that isn't meaningful to us, then we might succeed in the short term, but we will fail eventually.

I was referred to Gloria by her sister, who was concerned about the state of Gloria's apartment and about the fact that she had been evicted from her previous apartment for reasons related to the state of her belongings. Together, Gloria and I got the place in order, paring down the number of items and organizing them. Gloria and her sister were both very happy with the results.

But about six months later I saw Gloria's sister and asked how it was going. Gloria had completely reverted to her old habits, and her apartment had once again become dangerously cluttered. When I was there, Gloria's motivation had been driven by her eviction, her sister, and by me. But once I left, and the landlord left her alone, all she had was her sister's concern. (Obviously, that wasn't a major consideration.) She had no internal drive to stay organized. She was no longer motivated. So the stuff won.

☙ Success Factors ☚

A pattern that I've noticed is that several of my clients have engaged me after having gone through a significant weight loss. Marie Kondo reported a similar thing, but she saw the weight loss after the de-cluttering. Either way, a connection exists.

In my experience those clients who have gone through a successful weight loss are also the clients who have the most success in dealing with their excess stuff. They embrace the process more readily and they are better able to modify their habits to avoid accruing the superfluous items after I've gone.

This led me to think about that connection. Losing weight is all about self-control: eating healthy foods in moderate amounts and prioritizing exercise. Any other weight loss strategy will probably be unproductive. Controlling clutter is also all about self-control: taking the time to really look at belongings with a critical eye and make hard decisions about what to keep and what to release. The skills involved with doing one translate well to the other.

My client Martha had weight-related mobility issues when I originally helped her move from a house into a more comfortable condominium. The amount of stuff that had to be eliminated was staggering, but after the move her home was much easier to manage. Toward the end of that project, as I was hanging art on her walls, she invited me to join her for lunch, which she'd asked a friend to bring her: a large box of cake pops. I politely declined her offer.

Unfortunately, Martha's health issues escalated, so her brother-in-law called me back a year later to help her move to a care facility. The stuff in her home had increased, too, even though at that point she was completely bedridden. The junk hauler I brought in removed two more large truckloads of items for charity, recycling, and landfill.

Another connection to being organized is being successful. Studies have shown that people who make their beds every day are more successful than those who don't. I haven't seen any studies on it, but I suspect that the same may be true for people who put their dirty clothes in the laundry basket rather than on the floor.

❧ The Project ❧

Each client I've helped has followed a different path to get into his or her situation, which leads me to believe that each solution should also be unique. Many of my clients can only dedicate a few consecutive hours to clearing out before facing exhaustion and frustration. Other clients can tolerate three active 12-hour days in a row. Some clients have a hard deadline driving them, and others do not.

Interestingly, Marie Kondo and Margarete Magnussen have very different attitudes about this. Marie is convinced that the "correct" way to tidy a house is to do it all at once in a tremendous spurt of effort. Margarete, on the other hand, recommends a slow, steady approach.

My perspective is that the method should be what works best for the client, and that varies. However, I do always try to be reasonably systematic. I begin by working with the client to decide on a project sequence and a schedule, and then, to the extent possible, keep to that plan.

❧ The Plan ❧

As with any project, the first step is to decide what needs to be done. What is the goal, exactly? What will define success? Sometimes this is obvious and other times it's worth a discussion.

When I first started working with Valerie, she had planned a large dinner party, but had so much stuff in her dining area that her guests would have no place to sit. So, the initial goal was to make that dinner possible. Once that was done, and Valerie sent me pictures of the lovely dinner, then the goal changed. She and her significant other were so happy with their "new" dining area that the goal expanded to include other rooms in the house.

Once the goal is identified, the work plan takes shape, timing is estimated, and roles are assigned. Sometimes my own role is merely consultative: giving advice on process; providing recommendations on movers, junk haulers, and realtors; and lending a shoulder for crying. Other times, my role is more hands-on: personally packing items, directing contractor activities, and hauling charity donations.

❧ The Process ❧

Most projects involve sorting items in some way. Usually it involves multiple bags or boxes. Sometimes it involves defining "zones" on a table: charity on one end, recycling on the other, or some variation on that theme. Very often it involves loading charity items into the back of my car for transport to the local charity donation drop-off location.

In some cases, I find a spreadsheet useful. For example, Heloise had a huge house: seven bedrooms, eleven bathrooms, a spa, a pool, a greenhouse, a six-car garage, and so on. She and her husband had run a large business from their home. She also had several hundred works of art and dozens of pieces of antique furniture, including three grandfather clocks. In her case, I built a spreadsheet for each type of item, including where it was in the house and where it was going. We assigned catalog numbers to each piece of art and built an inventory.

Around that same time, I worked with another client whose move, including sorting, packing, and unpacking, was all done in one day. Her move was simple because she had so few belongings. Each move is different. The key to an efficient process is determining the scope of the work being done and tailoring the process to fit that type of work and scale of the effort involved.

❧ Categories of Items ☙

Although each client is different, the sorting process follows a common path. The first step is to decide which categories are relevant. In most cases, the client and I define at least four categories:

- Charity donations
- Recycling
- Landfill
- Keep

In some cases, these can be split into smaller designations. For example, some clients want clothing to go to one charity, electronics to another, and books to a third. The word "keep" is very general, too, and that category can be split in some circumstances. For clients who are moving but who own several houses, different "keep" items might be sent to different destinations.

Most clients have a few other categories, also. The most common is a category for a relative or two in another town or state. Another common category is consignment.

The consignment category usually triggers a difficult discussion. Once upon a time many antiques were valuable. A few still are, but not many. Also, the words "old" and "antique" do not have the same definition. This is a particularly difficult conversation when the client has held on to an old item because of its potential value on the antiques market. This often leads to disappointment, especially concerning furniture, china, crystal, and silver.

Clients frequently tell me exactly how much they had paid for an item, as if they would like me to get that money back for them. My response is to tell them what my mother said when I replaced a very worn carpet in my own home: "That old carpet didn't owe you nothin'." In other words, I had gotten good use out of that carpet for many years. That carpet had been fully depreciated a long time ago.

My client Molly had a fantastic collection of clothing, including beautiful designer gowns that she had worn to the opera and symphony. She had been acquiring them over the course of about 50 years and they were lovely. However, many of them had become moldy and moth-eaten, even though she had stored them fairly carefully. With brushing and pressing, I was able to salvage about half of them and then found a consigner who supplies Hollywood with period clothing. My client now receives a check from that consigner about once a year, and although that money is a tiny fraction of what she had spent, she sends the consigner a lovely thank-you note each time.

Once the categories are established, the client and I put together a color-coding system. I have my own preferences about colors (red for landfill, orange for recycling, and so on), but they really don't matter. What is important is to build a key and post it in a highly visible place wherever we are working. I use colored masking tape, mainly because it stays put but is easy to remove. Colored dots can work, but they tend to fall off of fabric and they're hard to remove from wood. I definitely advise against using post-it notes; they fall off of everything.

The tape will be used for marking large items, such as furniture and art. Physically moving the furniture into categories is usually impractical, so the tape is a quick way to keep track of decisions. I also like using tape to mark bags and boxes of smaller items. If the client is moving, items to keep often go into moving boxes as we sort. Those boxes will get colored tape AND labels indicating destination room and a summary of the contents.

This next idea may seem like a tiny detail, but it's important: In the sorting process, when I use masking tape, I have developed the habit of turning one end of the tape under by just a tiny bit. I do this even when I'm labelling moving boxes. That way, if any of us ends up having to remove that tape, we can just grab the turned-over end and pull. It's a time-saver.

Another detail is about labelling furniture. Many finishes and fabrics are pretty delicate, so I always make sure to put the tape where it won't pull anything away when it's removed.

❧ Sequence of Events ❧

Ideally, I like to start with clothing for a few reasons. It's easy, it builds confidence, it gets a rhythm going, and it gives me a chance to evaluate how realistic we've been about our timeframe. Both Marie and Margarete have come to the same conclusion.

Janelle's clothing was an obvious target because she had so much of it. She had an entire bedroom dedicated to black pants stored on rolling racks. Even if she wore a different pair of black pants every day, she wouldn't have had to repeat herself for years. Anyone could have found at least a few extraneous pairs of pants in that room.

But not every project can start with clothes. When I got to Gloria's apartment, the front (and only) door was blocked from the inside, so it would only open a few inches. Our first job was to clear a path so that we could pass in and out easily. Our second job was to deal with the smell: a jar of garlic olive oil had spilled in the kitchen and had oozed under other items that had been left on the kitchen floor, including clothing, books, toiletries, and so on. For my own comfort, dealing with that mess was a high priority.

Most projects do start with clothing. Letting go of clothes that no longer fit is actually a relief (especially if they are too small) and seeing the floor of the closet for the first time is a little thrill. It's also easy to understand how someone else can make good use of the item. Usually, sorting clothing is a pretty happy process.

From there, I suggest tackling whichever type of item seems easiest, then move down the categories, from easiest to hardest. This can vary pretty widely.

My client Petra asked me to help her clear out her house so that she could sell it after her husband had passed away. Her husband had lived there for about fifty years, but they had married late in life, so she had only lived there for about five years. She had already removed her own clothing and most of the pieces that she wanted to her new, smaller home, so what remained just needed sorting.

The furniture and décor items went to a charity, which came in with a large truck. That was the easy part. Her chosen charity was able to schedule a pickup within a week of our call. This was a big win, since charities sometimes require a month to six weeks lead time, or longer. Plus, most charities don't even bother going to rural areas.

In this case, the most difficult items were in the office. Petra's husband had been a cardiac surgeon and had collected medical books for a very long time. Petra felt strongly that those books should be useful to someone, so both she and I spent time looking for a library, bookstore, or medical facility that might be interested in them. Unfortunately, we both came up dry, so in the end that entire collection went to be recycled.

In most cases, books are one of the easier categories. A few clients have converted to e-books, so are willing to donate their paper books to charity. Others still like paper, but no longer read certain types of literature. More than once I've suggested to an elderly client that the chances of her reading *Ulysses* again are pretty slim.

Another point about books and other paper products is that they disintegrate. The glue that holds paperbacks together dries up and flakes off, so pages fall out. Old books, especially paperbacks, take on a sour smell after a while, too. Sometimes insects or rodents destroy them. So I encourage clients to donate those books as soon as they can so that someone can enjoy them before they start to fall apart or turn stinky.

The most difficult items are memorabilia, which I prefer to leave until last. These items often appear in the course of sorting other things, like clothes or books, and I usually set them aside to be handled at the end.

Because these items are so personal, I can't make many generalizations about them. I will simply say that they should constitute a very small percentage of a person's belongings. If the collection is disproportionately large, I'll counsel the client to reconsider his or her selections.

Nanette knew it would be difficult, so she asked me to go through her memorabilia with her. Even though I charge by the hour, she felt the time was worthwhile. She had a large drawer full of obituaries and other items related to the deaths of friends and family members. She wanted to pare that down to a small folder.

It was a long, difficult day for both of us, and the amount of space reclaimed was trivial. But Nanette felt better when it was over, and the following day felt positively joyous when we sorted through her cookbooks and recipe files!

My favorite memorabilia story concerns Heloise. I was working in her basement and ran across a very old scrapbook. It was covered in a thick layer of dust and the edges showed signs of having been chewed by some small critter. I dusted the scrapbook off and brought it upstairs to ask her about it.

As it turned out, that scrapbook documented Heloise's high school years, and she was very proud of it. She had me sit down and then walked me through the whole thing, including the plays she'd been in and the boy who had had a crush on her. Once we were was done, she closed the book, handed it back to me and said, "Now, toss that in the trash, then let's go scrub up because that thing is filthy!"

❧ Moving ❧

Frequently, the decluttering process occurs as part of a larger project: a move to a new residence. Even when it's not, some of the same issues, like packing and storage, still apply.

As I mentioned above, I'm a proponent of moving. I recognize that it's expensive and difficult, but it's often the best solution for a boatload of problems.

My mother-in-law had significant health issues when I met her in 1979, and those issues only increased over the years. My father-in-law took care of her until his own health began to deteriorate. Then we hired one, then two, caregivers. When the issues overcame their ability to cope, Mom and Dad moved into a senior community.

The good news is that their health immediately improved. They received better care from round-the-clock, professional staff. They ate meals designed by a nutritionist. Their rooms were safe and ADA-compliant. They had more frequent and more varied social interactions. They thrived in that environment, and probably lived longer than they would have at home. Just about all of my clients have similar stories about their moves. I only have two examples of clients who were unhappy about their moves.

The first was Marcella, who initially requested help moving from her condo to another condo in a nearby town. The project was going along fine until her grown children intervened and decided that she should instead move closer to one of them. Initially, she argued with them, but they eventually wore her down.

Several months after the move, Marcella called and said that she hated living in her son's town, and that the place where she lived made her feel like she was in prison. So, a few months after that, she relocated again, to the town where she had originally wanted to move.

The other client was unhappy because her new facility wouldn't let her continue to draw on multiple prescriptions for her medications.

The vast majority of clients find moving difficult, but life much better after the move. Even the unhappy clients were happy about moving, just not happy with their destination choices.

✺ Packing ✺

Quite a few of my clients feel the need to pack their own items. They believe that if they value items, they should pack them. My own opinion is quite the opposite. The movers that I am comfortable recommending are professionals. They do a much better and much more efficient job of wrapping and cushioning delicate items than the client could possibly do. They are also much less likely to drop or mishandle the boxes they've packed. Those men (and they are always men) are just bigger and stronger, and they haul boxes every day. Plus, they are very careful; they never lift more than they can handle safely.

Harriet had a large number of loose items in her apartment. Rather than using a chest of drawers, she stored her clothing in stacks around the bedroom. She had kept voluminous journals since her childhood, and so she had hundreds of handwritten notebooks stored in a random collection of boxes and tubs around the apartment. She designed and made jewelry, some of which had been displayed in a museum. She wanted to downsize, and since she had to move, the stuff had to be packed, but she was concerned. Rather than let the movers handle packing the "important" items, she asked me to wrap and pack them. More than half of her things fell into this category.

Interestingly, Harriet hired me again a year later. The new place hadn't worked out for her and she was repeating the process. Once again, I packed those "important" pieces extra-carefully, and hauled more extraneous items to charity. The process was far less efficient than it could have been, but Harriet was satisfied with it.

A critical fact to recognize is that moving is inherently a rough process. Even the most careful packing can result in damage. When breakage does occur, assigning liability is easier if the mover has both packed and transported the item.

Another client, Georgina, wanted me to start packing dishes immediately when I started working with her. But since she would continue to live (and eat) in the home for at least another week, I steered her toward starting by identifying items that she didn't plan to take with her to her new home.

So first we found new homes for two couches, a bed, a dining set, and so on. Then, the movers packed the dishes AFTER the house had been cleared of items that were not going to the new home. That way, she could use the dishes during the clearing process.

When the time came to pack the kitchen, Georgina told the movers to pack everything. So they did. She hadn't expected them to take her quite so literally, however. When she went in to make lunch, she discovered that they had already packed her loaf of bread.

❧ Movers ❧

Generally, movers can be placed into four categories:
- International
- National
- Local
- Guys with trucks

Often, international movers will take on national or local jobs, and national movers will take on local jobs if their schedules allow. But local movers may not have the wherewithal to take on an international or even a national move. National movers may not be able to handle international moves. These distinctions are usually pretty clear on the company's website, but if not, then a phone call is in order.

The "guys with trucks" category is tricky. This kind of company will almost definitely provide the lowest bid on a small move, and they could very well do a good job. But they are usually not bonded or insured, so if things go wrong, which can happen, then the financial implications could be significant. Moving companies pay very high insurance rates for a reason.

I generally recommend interviewing a few moving companies before deciding which one to use. My clients have all had different criteria for selecting their movers. I normally provide the client with a spreadsheet giving them the companies I know and what I know about each. Sometimes the client will select from that list, sometimes they will go with someone else's recommendation.

❧ Special Cases ☙

Some items require special attention. When they raise their ugly heads for the first time, figuring out how to deal with them takes a little bit of time. But, each time they appear, that category gets easier. Here are a few examples.

❧ Automobiles ❧

Automobiles are occasionally part of the clutter in a house, especially when one member of the household has passed away. In those cases, the car may have been sitting idle for quite some time, slowly becoming one with the earth. I've seen trees growing through floorboards.

In those cases, the options include salvage yards and recycling centers. Since I am less than expert on the value of older cars, I usually take photos to get a more informed opinion of the best approach. That set of photos includes the vehicle identification number (VIN) which is right in front of the windshield on the driver's side.

On the other end of the spectrum was the Lexus that had been sitting in Heloise's garage for several years. It was hooked up to a tricklecharger, so the battery wasn't dead, and once in a while some member of Heloise's family would drive it around town for an afternoon.

When the garage needed to be emptied, I made a call to a local car dealership and talked to the used car sales department. The car was valuable, so the dealership sent a representative out to Heloise's home to inspect the car, evaluate its condition, take a test drive, and make an offer. In the end, the car remained in Heloise's family, but the experience was overall positive, and I would not hesitate to request that service from that dealership again.

Another good option is the vehicle donation process. Many charities now accept donations of cars, trucks, boats, RVs, and so on. I've only done this once, and it went fairly well. The charity picked up the vehicle and all seemed well. However, a few months later, the old owner received a notification that the car had received a parking ticket. Apparently, the charity had not yet completed the paperwork on the transfer of the vehicle. Surprisingly, this was simple to resolve through the Department of Motor Vehicles (DMV).

In whatever way the automobile question is resolved, the DMV needs to know about it and the transfer must be finalized with them.

❧ China, Silver, and Crystal ❧

I've mentioned these items before, but they're worth a little more discussion here. Years ago, these were highly desired items that one expected to collect very slowly over one's lifetime and pass down through the generations. That horse has left the barn.

Handmade porcelain dishware is very expensive and quite delicate. Chips and breaks are disastrous. Modern, inexpensive dishes can be very attractive. If an entire table setting of attractive, inexpensive dishes can be purchased for less than one piece of handmade porcelain, which would be a more logical choice for a rowdy Thanksgiving dinner? So, the trend today is away from the high-end items to the more practical alternatives.

The same is true for crystal and silver. However, in the case of silver, the metal itself has some value. I have taken silver pieces to a shop near me that will melt it down and pay for it by the ounce. I'm also aware of some artists who turn silverware into jewelry.

I should point out, however, that silver candlesticks are often weighted with an internal core of concrete, which has to be removed before the melting process. The cost of doing that usually offsets the value of the silver, resulting in no advantage in the whole effort.

❧ Drugs ❧

In my line of work, I rarely run across illegal drugs, and I'm not sure I would recognize them if I did, but I almost always encounter prescription drugs, over-the-counter drugs, herbal medicines, and so on. In one case, I ran across an entire coat closet filled with unopened packages of Viagra AND Cialis.

I'm fortunate in that a drugstore near my home has a bin in which I can deposit unused medications, which they will then destroy. This is a much better solution than sending them to a landfill or pouring them down the drain.

❧ Hazardous Materials ❧

Most moving companies refuse to haul any items that can cause problems in transit. One of those problems is fire, so anything flammable probably will need special handling. Because alcohol is flammable, I usually recommend that the client have a big party before the move to minimize the amount of alcohol that needs to be moved. If the move is local, what's left can go in a box in the trunk of a car.

Other common fire hazards include:

- Cleaning supplies
- Art supplies
- Charcoal starter
- Propane

The best approach is to use common sense. If the item could explode or catch on fire, it should probably be handled with care.

I'm lucky in that our local recycling center has a hazardous waste disposal service that is free and easy to use, so rather than worrying about transporting these items, I usually recommend disposing of them and buying new products as needed after the move. This is especially true when the item in question is more than a few years old.

One item that might seem counterintuitive is the fire extinguisher. Its contents are under extreme pressure, so if it is crushed or punctured it could explode or accidentally discharge. Neither would be good. My advice is to leave it and buy a new one for the new home.

❧ Firearms ❧

Even the strongest anti-gun activists sometimes have guns in their homes. Occasionally, other members of that household are unaware of their presence, which can lead to surprises after a death in the family.

In most cases, however, the firearms are known, well-secured, and handled properly. Petra's home had gun racks on the walls, so I expected to find guns. But, as it turned out, her husband had dealt with them in his final years. I just had to dis-mantle the racks. Then, as we went through his desk, we found what looked like a very tiny gun, but which on closer inspection turned out to be an antique starter pistol.

Generally, however, my process for dealing with guns starts with making sure that the gun isn't loaded. Then, I'll put it in its case, if it isn't there already. If the client wants to sell the gun, I make an appointment with a local gun dealer. Firearms laws vary considerably by jurisdiction, so a local dealer is a good resource. If no dealer is available, then I would contact the local firearms licensing authority.

The dealer will provide an estimated value and the client can then decide whether to sell it through that dealer. Some clients prefer to transfer the ownership to another family member, which the dealer can also facilitate.

Another option, which I've only used once, is a government buy-back program. These programs usually only run for one day and are very infrequent. But if the timing works, they can be good news for the client, because the purchase prices that governments offer are usually not tied to the value of that particular gun, which could be quite low. So, those programs can be a good deal for the low-value gun owner.

My favorite firearms story is about the cannon Carol had. Her husband had been a lawyer, and his firm celebrated court victories by firing the cannon. Carol was happy to let the cannon go.

❦ Pets ❧

Quite a few clients of mine have had pets, and some of them have presented unique challenges. I have a wonderful friend who is a vet who makes house calls, which has made a big difference a few times. I've also recommended a couple of different boarding facilities for pets during the transition to a new home. The idea is to reduce stress for both the people and the pets.

Heloise had a cat named Fang. (That's the one name in this book that I didn't invent. That was really his name. He would bite anyone who tried to touch him.) I don't think that Fang knew that he belonged to Heloise, because he came and went as he pleased. He had been neutered when he was very young but had not had any shots or medical care since then. He was basically a feral cat, hugely overweight, wormy, and flea-infested. But Heloise loved him and wanted to take him with her when she moved.

I started with by having my friend bring Fang's shots up to date. Then I called the Feral Cat Society to get their advice on transporting Fang. To my surprise, they offered to come out and help with Fang and show me how to handle feral cats. Fortunately, by that time, Fang had become accustomed to me, so I was one of the few people he would allow to touch him. It turned out to be a piece of cake.

Then there was the saltwater aquarium. It was elaborate and expensive, so I had expected that some school or hospital would be delighted to receive it as a gift. We called all over town without any luck.   Fortunately, the man who had been coming to clean and service the tank was willing to help.   He had his own tank at home and agreed to make room there for just a few more aquatic residents.

❧ Pornography ☙

Another special category is pornography, which I do run across once in a while. It's often embarrassing to the person who has hired me, because they hadn't even known it was there. For example, Roland hired me after his dad had a stroke, and the home care provider that Roland had hired for him was not working out well. My job was to sort through Dad's things and pack what he would need to take with him to the care facility that Roland had found for him.

We discovered that Roland's dad had a collection of videotapes that he had never shared with his son. The covers were pretty graphic. Roland and I agreed that regardless of Dad's preferences, we would destroy the tapes rather than send them on to his dad's new home. He was going to have to make do with his collection of James Bond and other action films, and the staff of the care facility wouldn't have to see the pornography.

When my children were young, they referred to me as KJ (for Kill Joy) because I never let them do anything remotely fun, like jumping off of the roof. My KJ recommendation is to simply destroy the pornography without further ado. In most cases, it's in the home because a teenager stashed it in a hiding place years ago and forgot about it.

❧ Toys ☙

This is a broad category, spanning golf clubs to model trains to fishing equipment to bicycles. Many of these items are a challenge, because new ones are quite expensive and selling used ones is a project. As with many other expensive items, the question is whether the amount of money gained is worth the cost of the time that selling them requires. Someone who has more time than money may decide that the effort is worthwhile, but that has not been the case for very many of my clients.

One exception to this was William's boat. He was determined to sell it, so I listed it online for him. When a buyer contacted me, I arranged to show him the boat. I did this with some trepidation, because the boat was in a fairly remote location and I had no way of knowing if the buyer was sincere or had some kind of nefarious intention. But it all turned out well and the sale went through at the price William had established. However, I would hesitate to do that again.

My favorite place to take bicycles is a local organization called Trips for Kids, which organizes bike rides in the country for inner city kids. They take old bikes and fix them up, selling some and using others for their trips.

Model trains are fairly common in my experience, too, and I'm happy to report that we have a local hobby shop willing to find good homes for them. Hearing how much a child appreciates a train is sometimes compensation enough.

If the toy might be collectible, the owner could have relevant contacts worth checking. If not, a local club may be able to help. However, in my experience, toys very rarely have any collectible value.

❧ Maintenance ❧

"It's a river." – Libby Wood

My client Valerie told me that this was the most important thing that I told her.

We can't keep everything. No filing system can accommodate every item we love that passes through our homes. We can't possibly keep every magazine we ever receive or even every cartoon that has made us laugh. We need to appreciate them, then let them go.

Recognizing that we can't keep everything forces us to get what we can out of it while we have it. If we say to ourselves that we can always refer back to this booklet (if we can find it), then we don't need to remember what is in it. But, if we know that we are going to give away or recycle the booklet, then we HAVE to remember what it says.

The key is to know which items to keep and which to let go. Periodically reviewing the items in the home keeps the river from being a stagnant pond. Here are a few questions to ask when making that distinction regarding the clothing, books, magazines, newspapers (and newspaper clippings) that make up the river:

Clothes:
- Does it fit perfectly?
- Does it look great on me?
- Will I really mend it? Today? This week?
- Can I really get that stain out?

- Is it really still in fashion?

Books and magazines:

- Will I read it again? When?
- Is it in good condition?
- Does it smell?
- Could someone else get more enjoyment out of it now than I will in the future?

Marie Kondo recommends asking if it sparks joy, which is a great question, too. Those mortgage documents probably don't do that, but I think she'd understand keeping them around. She'd probably also understand that even if a book sparked joy when I read it, I will NOT keep it around unless I'm sure that I want to reread it soon.

Another point about clothes is that "around the house" clothing isn't regular clothing that got downgraded. If we spill spaghetti sauce on our evening clothes, we don't relegate those clothes to "around the house" status. The same is true for business clothes that no longer fill that purpose. We should have casual wear that was purchased for that purpose and is comfortable and tidy.

I keep a grocery bag on the floor of my closet. Then, after a long day of wearing shoes that pinch, I can take them off and put them straight into the bag. When it's full, the whole bag goes to charity so that someone with smaller feet can love those shoes. The same goes for blouses that gap, sweaters that are pilled, and T-shirts that have shrunk.

Even if those items are in terrible shape, many charities have fiber reclamation processes, so that the fibers in the clothing can be reused even if the clothes themselves are too far gone to wear. So I don't worry about distinguishing between items that can be resold and those that can't.

I have a book bag, too. I only have so much room for books

by my bed, and usually have a few books in process at any given time. (Yes, I admit to liking real paper books.) But I remove books from that shelf once I've read them and put them in my "Friends of the Library" bag. I almost never read books more than once, although I do confess to keeping quite a few old math and science textbooks, just because I like the way they explain certain concepts.

I always have a stack of magazines ready to take with me to the beauty salon. I remove my address label, then add them to the pile on their coffee table. Once in a while that pile moves from there down the road to a senior facility which uses them once more before the paper gets recycled.

I keep a basket in the kitchen for newspapers, too. Although we have a door-to-door recycling service, I prefer to take those newspapers to Guide Dogs for the Blind, which shreds them and uses them for the puppies. Getting rid of things is easier for me when I know that someone else, especially a puppy, is going to make good use of it.

❧ Storage ❧

"A place for everything and everything in its place."
— 17th Century wisdom

Entire store chains have been built to serve our need for storage. We're tempted to think that if we just buy enough bins, we can contain all of our excess stuff. Putting our stuff out of sight in those bins feels good, and when we're done, we feel like we've made progress. But have we?

I can't tell you how many bins I've opened with my clients, without their knowing beforehand what is inside. Sometimes it's like Christmas: "I wondered where that went!" But much more often it's a disappointment: "Why one earth did I save that?!"

I'm not against storage bins; I actually love them. Finding one that is exactly the right size and shape, that closes tightly, is a joy. They are terrific at keeping out vermin and corralling smaller items. But we need to be very thoughtful about when and where to use them. We need to be sure that they are the right solution for the problem at hand.

We also need to be aware of the cost of storage. Renting a storage unit at $100/month would cost $1,200/year or $12,000 for ten years. Is this a good value for what is being stored?

Even if the items can be stored in the home, that storage involves a cost. When garages can't be used for cars because they are filled with dusty exercise bikes and baby furniture, then the cars have to sit outside in the weather, which prematurely ages them. When kitchen counters are so cluttered with old mail and newspapers that they can't be used for cooking, fast food and frozen dinners become the only viable options. A closet filled with shoe boxes full of golf balls can't be used for anything else.

Often when cleaning out closets, clients will find items that they thought they had lost or didn't know that they had. Sometimes they had gone out and purchased replacement items. Sometimes they had done that more than once. Overstuffed storage can be expensive.

So, what kind of items are appropriate to put in storage? The answer is: items that definitely will be used, just not right now. Some examples of this are:

- Seasonal clothing: winter clothes in summer and summer clothes in winter
- Holiday décor items that we actually use for Christmas, Halloween, Easter, etc.
- Tire chains that fit a current vehicle

Baby items can also go on this list, too, with a few caveats. Not only do styles change dramatically over the years, so do safety features. A crib that was perfectly fine when I was a child would be viewed with horror today. (Actually, my crib was a banana box, and it doubled as my car seat in the days before mandatory seat belts and car seats.) So, children's items can be stored for short periods of time, but, really, a better solution is to donate them right away to a children's consignment store or a charity.

Items that are NOT appropriate for storage include:

- Tire chains that DON'T fit a current vehicle
- Broken appliances, radios, and TVs
- Magazines and books
- Unfinished art projects and their components

Before I retired from my corporate career, I often thought that once I did retire, I would fill my days with all kinds of little art projects. So, I tucked away bits and pieces of things that would be useful. When that day actually came, and I had the time to tackle those projects, I pulled them out of the cupboard and started asking myself, "What was I thinking?" Those little things no longer inspired me, and I found myself much more interested in new projects and ideas. So, I passed my stuff along, the same way that I now encourage my clients to do.

The broken appliance collection is a pet peeve of mine. I've seen garages so full of old, broken appliances that almost nothing else could be stored there, including automobiles. The appliances were so old that even if they were fixed, no one would want them, but not so old as to be museum exhibits. The space was completely wasted.

Many of us remember the days when an appliance lasted a very long time and was repeatedly repaired when parts failed. Modern appliances have a shorter lifespan. When an appliance is replaced, the old one should be recycled.

❧ Order Out of Chaos ☙

"Art, in itself, is an attempt to bring order out of chaos."
– Stephen Sondheim

We also have a need for storage for the things we use every day. For these things, we don't need bins, we need accessible closets and chests. We need to organize them so that they work well for us and follow a system that is easy to maintain.

Harriet had quite a bit of stuff, but she lacked storage. Her clothing was in stacks on the floor in the bedroom and in tubs around her apartment. The disarray appealed to her sense of artistic disorder, but it was difficult to manage. She spent quite a bit of time bouncing around her place looking for things.

My own recommendation is to be thoughtful and realistic about storage needs. Anyone with a small apartment will find 300 sweaters difficult to manage and will struggle to find furniture that not only holds all of them but fits in the space. This isn't a complicated math problem. So I'd suggest finding furniture that reasonably fits the living space and holds as much as possible. Then pare down the clothing and other items to fit neatly into that furniture.

I recommend following a modified Marie Kondo approach to folding and storing items in drawers. Most items are best stored folded into a small rectangle then placed vertically in the drawer, so that when the drawer is open all of its contents are visible. It's neat and tidy, easy to do, and holds more that stacking them in horizontal layers.

One exception to this is the way I store scarves, which I keep loose in a basket in my closet. I also disagree with her approach to purses or handbags (or pocketbooks as my college roommate called them). Marie recommends storing them nested one inside the other. The ones I'm not using sit alone and rather forlorn on the top shelf of my closet waiting for me to use them. Of course, I only own four purses, and carry the same one almost all the time.

꧁ The Pursuit of Happiness ꧂

"Happiness is a warm puppy." – Charles Schulz

We all define happiness in different ways. A few years ago, I went to a panel discussion about happiness, with each of the participating researchers coming at the topic from a different perspective. One of the things I learned was that studies have shown that people's assessments of their own overall happiness change as they age, and those changes tend to follow a common pattern. Their happiness levels drop after youth, then increase from their fifties through their seventies.

Part of why this is true may be that older people have learned how to "not sweat the small stuff" in life. Experience has taught them how to deal with various forms of adversity and to be content. But contentment is not the same as complacency.

As we age, small stuff can become bigger. Home maintenance projects become more difficult, and so we choose to overlook maintenance issues. We put a pitcher under the leaky faucet rather than getting the problem fixed. We avoid the sagging floorboards. We do creative things with duct tape. Those small accommodations accumulate, and we find ourselves in a very uncomfortable place.

We struggle more with mobility and accessibility as we age, too. Stairs are harder to climb. Taking the garbage out to the street is a heavier burden. Stepping in and out of a bathtub can become an ordeal. Bathmats become slipping hazards.

Most of my clients are over 50. Many of them have had a major life event that has triggered them to recognize the need for change. Often that's a death, but occasionally it's an eviction. Once it was a fire. But my favorite clients are those who realize that they would just be happier with a simpler, more organized living space.

My own theory is that part of being happy at any stage in life depends partially upon being comfortable in one's environment. If that environment is uncomfortable, then changing it is important, even if that change is painful. The longer we allow the status quo to continue, the more difficult and painful that change becomes.

To manage that environment successfully, sometimes we just have to be brave.